Cumbria Libraries

D0316064

Hidden in
the Grass

Barbara Taylor

QED
QED Publishing

Front cover: A lion is well hidden among the long, dry grass of its African home.

Project Editor: Angela Royston
Designer: Matthew Kelly
Picture Researcher: Maria Joannou

Copyright © QED Publishing 2011

First published in the UK in 2011 by
QED Publishing
A Quarto Group Company
226 City Road
London EC1V 2TT

www.qed-publishing.co.uk

The words in **bold** are explained in the Glossary on page 22.

All rights reserved. No part of this publication may be reproduced, stored in a retrieval system, or transmitted in any form or by any means, electronic, mechanical, photocopying, recording, or otherwise, without the prior permission of the publisher, nor be otherwise circulated in any form of binding or cover other than that in which it is published and without a similar condition being imposed on the subsequent purchaser.

A catalogue record for this book is available from the British Library.

ISBN 978 1 84835 609 2

Printed in China

Picture credits
(t=top, b=bottom, l=left, r=right, fc=front cover, bc=back cover)
Corbis Joe McDonald 1, 12, Stuart Corlett 13b, Theo Allofs 15b; **FLPA** Frank Stober/ Imagebroker 4, Donald M. Jones/Minden Pictures 11, Edward Myles 13t, Paul Hobson 15t, Imagebroker 17t; **Nature Picture Library** Nature Production 5t, Tom Vezo 7t, Pete Oxford 7b, Andy Sands 19t, Robin Chittenden 19b, Paul Johnson 20t, Wild Wonders of Europe/Shpilen 20b, Sinclair Stammers 21t; **Photolibrary** Panthera Productions/ABPL 5b, Peter Arnold Images/Martin Harvey 6, Michel & Christine Denis-Huot 8–9, Animals Animals/Miriam Agron 10l, All Canada Photos/ Ron Erwin 10r, Index Stock Imagery/William Ervin 14, Geoff Higgins 18, Age Fotostock/David Cappaert 21b; **Shutterstock** EcoPrint fc and bc, Cederlund Thorlin 2-3, lloyd s clemens 16-17, Lockenes 22-23, Jakub Gruchot 24.

LIBRARY SERVICES
FOR SCHOOLS

380060430056746

Bertrams   31/01/2012

591.47   £4.99

LSS

Contents

Hiding in the grass

big, round ears to listen for danger

Animals that live in hot or cool **grasslands** are good at hide and seek. The animals hide by blending in with the background. This is called **camouflage**.

Many grassland animals are hard to see because they have patterns on their fur or feathers. African wild dogs have brown, black and white fur. They are sometimes called painted dogs!

long, strong legs for chasing after other animals

◄ Every African wild dog has a different pattern on its fur.

Green or brown?

When there is plenty of rain, grasses are green. Some animals, such as grasshoppers, are green to match the green grass. This makes it hard for enemies to spot them, especially when they keep still.

When the weather is very dry, the grass turns brown. Some grassland animals, such as lions, are brown. This colour hides them when they hunt in the dry grass.

HIDE AND SEEK

Can you see the grasshopper hiding in the green grass?

▼ Lions need to be very well camouflaged to get close to the animals they hunt.

good eyesight

brown fur matches the dry grass

ears that hear the quietest sounds

Hunting in the grass

Large **herds** of animals such as zebras **graze** on hot, grassy lands. Lions, hyenas and other animals hunt these large herds. Many animals hunt at night when it is cooler.

The hunters are called **predators**. The animals they hunt are their **prey**. Spotted hyenas hunt in **packs**. They work together to kill animals as large as a zebra or even a buffalo.

spotted fur

eyes that see well in the dark

strong legs for running fast

▲ Hyenas can make lots of strange sounds, including yells, whoops and scary laughing calls.

Daytime hunters

During the day, prairie falcons fly low to the ground to catch birds and ground squirrels. Their streaked and spotted brown feathers blend in with the landscape.

sharp beak for tearing flesh from prey

long tail feathers help bird to steer when flying

ANIMAL TALK

- Female hyenas lead the pack.
- Male boomslangs can be green, black or blue, but females are always brown.

▼ A boomslang hides among the leaves of a small tree.

Lying in wait

Boomslang snakes don't mind the heat. They lie in wait until they spot a lizard or bird to eat. Then they strike suddenly and kill their prey with a poisonous bite.

Speedy spotted cats

The cheetah's spotted fur blends into a background of tall grasses. This helps the cheetah to get close to its prey during the day, when other predators are sleeping in the shade.

A cheetah preys on herds of animals, such as gazelles. The cheetah creeps up and then attacks quickly. It chooses a small gazelle and sprints after it.

long tail for balance and steering while turning fast

sharp claws for gripping the ground like running shoes

powerful back legs and large muscles for running fast

Fastest in the world

Cheetahs are the fastest **mammals** in the world. They can sprint at up to 112 kilometres per hour! But they can run fast for only a short distance – like an Olympic sprinter. If they don't catch their prey quickly, they get too hot and have to stop running to cool down.

▼ A cheetah chases a young gazelle. A cheetah can go from standing still to 96 kilometres per hour in just three seconds!

CHEETAH FACTS

- Every cheetah has a different pattern of spots on its coat.

- Cheetahs do not roar like lions or tigers, but they purr like a pet cat.

Hiding from hunters

Grasslands are so dry that few trees can grow here. There are not many places for hunted animals to hide. Camouflage helps them to stay alive!

Prairie dogs live in **burrows**, which they dig below ground. They come out during the day to feed on grass, seeds and flowers. Their brown fur blends with the brown soil around their burrows.

▼ If a predator appears, the prairie dogs quickly disappear underground.

big eyes for spotting danger

brown and grey fur

sharp claws for digging holes

Two colours

Pronghorn antelopes are brown on top and white below. When the sunlight shines on them, their round bodies look flat. This makes the antelopes hard to see from a distance. If predators such as wolves get close, the pronghorns run away very fast.

males have large horns for fighting

good eyesight for seeing predators far away

◀ Pronghorns live on the grassy lands of North America.

ANIMAL TALK

- Prairie dogs are named after their barking call, which sounds like a dog.

- Pronghorns are the second fastest animals on land, after the cheetah.

Eggs, chicks and babies

Grasslands have only a few trees, so many birds lay their eggs on the ground. Several ostriches share a nest. They lay their eggs in the same small dip in the ground.

During the day, one female sits on all the eggs to keep them warm. Her brown feathers camouflage her. At night, a male ostrich sits on the eggs. His black feathers hide him in the dark.

long neck for seeing predators over the tall grasses

▲ A female ostrich is well camouflaged as she sits on the eggs.

large body, which is too heavy for the bird to fly

▼ A blue crane chick is better camouflaged than its mother.

Baby colours

Blue crane chicks have light and dark brown fluffy feathers. These colours camouflage them in the dry grass.

Baby animals are small and easy for predators to catch when their mothers are out hunting. Lion cubs are spotted all over to hide them from hunters.

ANIMAL TALK

• Ostriches are the largest birds in the world and lay the largest eggs.

• A female lion licks her cubs so they all have the same scent.

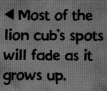

◀ Most of the lion cub's spots will fade as it grows up.

Patches and stripes

Many animals search for food early in the morning or late in the evening. Their stripes and patches help to hide them among the patches of light and long, dark shadows.

very long neck to reach food high in the trees

The patches on a giraffe's fur look like broken paving stones. These animals disappear into the shadows of the trees.

◄ Giraffes feed on the leaves of trees and rest in their shade.

Stripy patterns

A corncrake's stripy brown feathers match the grass stems. When a corncrake crouches in the grass and keeps very still, it is almost impossible to see.

▼ A corncrake comes out at dawn and dusk to feed on insects.

HIDE AND SEEK

Can you see the baby anteater riding piggyback on its mother's back? It looks like part of its mother!

The giant anteater's black and white stripes blend into the long grass when it hunts for **insects** to eat.

Stripy zebras

A zebra's vertical stripes break up its shape. Herds of zebras just fade into the grassy background. Predators cannot see where one zebra ends and another zebra begins.

Lions see everything in black and white – they cannot see colours. This makes it harder for lions to see a particular zebra against a grassy background.

ZEBRA FACTS

- Zebras are black with white stripes (not white with black stripes!)
- Zebras can walk, trot, canter and gallop, just like horses.

Narrow escapes

Lions like to pick out one zebra that looks old, weak or injured, because it will be easier to catch. But when lions attack, zebras run in all directions.

The lions are confused by all the moving stripes. They may attack a strong animal by mistake, or they may jump the wrong way.

▲ Zebras keep close together when they drink in case a lion tries to attack them.

good hearing to listen for danger

eyes on sides of head to see all around

◄ Herds of zebras and antelopes often graze together. They help each other to watch out for predators.

Invisible insects

All kinds of tiny insects hide in the grass under the feet of the big grassland animals.

A green praying mantis is almost invisible when it keeps really still. This keeps it safe from predators such as birds and bats. It also helps it to make surprise attacks on other insects.

big front legs for grabbing prey

strong jaws for crunching prey

spikes on legs for gripping prey

▲ A praying mantis tiptoes along a stem of grass.

Dull underneath

Butterflies close their wings when they rest, so the undersides of their wings are camouflaged. The white wings of orange tip butterflies are green and black underneath. These colours hide them when they rest.

▼ The wings of blue butterflies have bright colours on top but are brown below.

▲ An orange tip butterfly rests on a flower.

ANIMAL TALK

• A praying mantis eats its prey while it is still alive!

• The orange colour on a male orange-tip butterfly warns predators that it is poisonous.

wings covered with tiny coloured scales

false eye

antennae for smelling, touching and tasting

False eyes

A long-tailed blue butterfly has spots that look like eyes at the tip of its wings. A predator is tricked into attacking the false eyes instead of the butterfly's body. The butterfly needs its body, but can live without a small piece of its wing.

Changing Colour

Some animals change colour if the background changes colour. Some grasslands are dry in summer, but covered with snow in winter.

Saiga antelopes are brown in summer. In winter, they grow thick, white fur to camouflage them against the white snow.

▼ A saiga antelope has a long, floppy nose. Its nose keeps out dry dust in summer and warms the air it breathes in winter.

males have long horns for fighting

▲ A saiga antelope's white fur blends in with the winter snow.

long, rubbery nose, like a short elephant-trunk

long legs for running fast

Matching the flowers

Many female crab spiders change colour to match different flowers growing in grassy meadows. Spiders need to match the flowers, so they can wait for their prey without being seen.

Crab spiders get their name because they move sideways, like a crab.

HIDE AND SEEK

Crab spiders do not make webs. They change colour to hide among the flowers instead. Can you spot the crab spider on this white flower?

long front legs act like pincers to grasp prey

poisonous fangs for biting prey

▶ A crab spider can take up to three days to change colour. Its body makes the new colours.

Glossary

burrow a long tunnel dug in the soil by animals such as prairie dogs.

camouflage Colours, patterns or markings that help an animal to hide by matching the background.

grasslands Large areas of land where grasses are the main plants. Grasslands grow in places that are too dry for forests but too wet for deserts.

graze To eat plants, usually grasses.

herd A group of hoofed mammals that feed and move around together.

insect A small animal with six legs and three parts to its body.

mammal An animal that has hair or fur on its body and drinks its mother's milk when young.

pack A group of hunting animals, such as African wild dogs.

predator An animal that hunts and kills other animals to get food to eat.

prey An animal hunted and killed by a predator.

Did you spot them?
The grasshopper on page 5 is in the centre of the photo. On page 15, the baby anteater looks like a bump on its mother's back. The spider on page 21 is lighter than the flower petals and its legs look like crab's claws.

Index

Notes for parents and teachers

As you share this book with children, ask questions to encourage them to look closely at the detail in the photographs.

What is grass?

- Explain to the children that grasses are made up of a mass of shallow underground roots and green shoots above ground.
- Help the children to grow their own grass from seeds on a small dish or plate. Remember: grass needs soil, water and sun to grow! Help them lay out soil, sow the seeds and ensure the soil is watered regularly and that the dish stands in a light spot. If grass does not have enough water it turns dry and brown.

Hunters and hunted

- Look through the book and ask the children to find the predators (hunters) and prey (hunted animals).
- Animals that live in groups, such as zebras or lions, help each other to watch out for danger and find food. Children can also help to look out for each other! Talk to the children about teamwork and how groups of people help each other, too.

Moving around

- Camouflage works best when animals keep still, but sometimes they have to run away from predators and other dangers, such as grassland fires.
- Fast-running animals on grasslands usually have long legs, which also help them to see over the tops of tall grasses.

Spots and stripes

- Many grassland animals have spots or stripes, which blend in well with the shadows at dawn or dusk, when many hunters are about. This makes both predators and prey hard to see in the dim light. Can the children think of any other animals that have spots and stripes?

Big and small animals

- Both tiny insects and big lions need camouflage to help them survive, but camouflage is more important for the smaller, weaker insects, which are less able to defend themselves.
- Amazingly, the huge numbers of tiny insects living on grasslands eat far more overall than the large herds of grazing animals.